eCEM© - effective Cyber Exposure Management

Fourth Edition

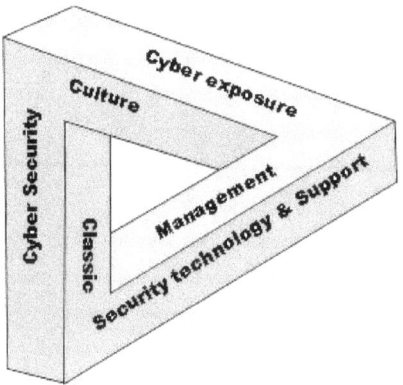

Douglas A. Nagan.

DEDICATION

This book is dedicated to all those who are combating cyber exposures.

ACKNOWLEDGMENTS

This book could not have been written without the help of Anne Nagan for her editing prowess, Ned Dunham for providing his insights into non technical cyber risks and Don Eckenfelder for his advocacy regarding the importance of understanding and managing culture.

Table of Contents

Introduction to the 4th Edition

This edition includes my current thinking regarding how to address and manage the exposures and risks present in the cyber eco-systems we all inhabit. The activities of the predators that inhabit these cyber eco-system continually evolve and mutate to take advantage of weaknesses and vulnerabilities. While there are occasional activities aimed at disrupting an organization in the main their objective is to make money with as little effort as possible. Which means in the main one of your key strategies must be to not be easy prey.

Make no mistake about it this is a never ending battle that will require constant attention, resources and time for the forseeable future.

We have constructed the material into three main sections for ease of use and reference:

1. Getting your strategy right
2. Understanding all your cyber exposures
3. Managing your efforts

As part of this we have added new material on managing cyber exposures throughout the book.

The new figure on the cover, and shown below, illustrates the three main activities that a successful cyber exposure management program must include.

- Classic Security Technology &Support
- Cyber Exposure Management
- A Robust Cyber Security Culture

Each of these is necessary but not sufficient for an effective program. And the use of an Escher shape helps make the point that they are all intertwined and rely on each other in ways that are not always apparent.

We cannot guarantee using this book will protect you from all the cyber predators, or a dysfunctional culture, but the information herein will help guide you from becoming easy prey.

Be safe and be secure.

What is effective Cyber Exposure Management (eCEM©)

In 2018 the pace of change in malicious cyber events is accelerating. In the past the risks were mainly in someone gaining access to valuable information such as proprietary company information, financial records, customer credit card data, and similar information and then using the information for gain. We are now seeing a rise in harming the ability of an organization, or an individual, to function by disabling key operations, and sometimes demanding a ransom payment to return it to normal. Additionally there is a rise in malicious exposures to harm a company's repute. A recent example is the Sony hack. To effectively address this you need to understand the distinction between cyber risks and cyber exposure which will inevitably lead to a change in how your cyber exposures are addressed.

Cyber exposures are the vulnerabilities that arise when you use cyber technology. They are ignored at your peril. This book will provide you with guidance on how to identify and manage your cyber exposures.

It is our experience that an eCEM© program can contribute to the bottom line not only by lessening losses but by improving organizational efficiency and effectiveness. This book shows you how.

What is cyber exposure management, and why not call it cyber risk management? The reason is that the term cyber risk implies a technical issue whereas in our opinion, the issue is much broader and includes human behavior issues, use of social media, your cyber culture, legal, compliance and intellectual property exposures as well as other related exposures. Also the term exposure, as opposed to risk, is closer to defining the situation. Risk implies a known threat whereas exposure implies a vulnerability to potential harm which may be undefined and unknown. We will expand on this in Section 2.

The concepts behind effective Cyber Exposure Management (eCEM©) build on those in our prior book eERM©- effective Enterprise Risk Management[1]. Cyber exposure management can be viewed as a subset of Enterprise Risk Management. However the unique properties of cyber exposure warrant a separate document focused on cyber issues and how best to address them. If you have read eERM© you will find several of the key concepts reiterated and restated. As much as we would like you to have read eERM, though it is not required to understand and apply the concepts put forward in this book as you address your cyber exposures.

Our objective is to provide guidance to those who have the overall responsibility for an organization concerning cyber exposure. We will do this by providing a framework to understand cyber exposure and how to manage your approach. This book is not a technical primer on technologies to combat, or lessen, cyber exposure. Rather a management strategy on how to identify and manage your cyber exposure.

The reason for this is that your biggest exposures are likely not from technical failures[2] but rather from mundane failures such as:

- Un disciplined use of social media (i.e. – those pictures of the office party would never have been seen by the board)
- Not understanding the exposures involved in the Internet of Things (IoT)
- Not encrypting data in transit (i.e. – if the memory stick left in the cab had been encrypted the 10,000 client records could not have been read by your competitor)
- Not paying attention to password security (i.e. – not changing default passwords or making your password 'PASSWORD")

---

[1] ISBN 978-1460980446 available through Amazon

[2] Verizon 2012 Data Breach Investigations Report

- Being unaware of the legal liabilities arising from intellectual property misuse or the hidden pitfalls in cloud computing contracts.
- Compliance failure to protect personal information

'effective Cyber Exposure Management' (eCEM©) is an expansion of the approach of identifying, assessing, measuring, monitoring, mitigating or transferring (as appropriate), and generally managing the cyber exposure an enterprise is exposed to either deliberately or accidentally. eCEM© matters because the corporate highway is littered with a legion of maimed and slain bodies of enterprises who failed this vital management practice. Unfortunately much of this carnage could have been avoided by applying some basic principles and avoiding known major pitfalls.

This document will be useful to both the cyber exposure practitioner as well as senior management by examining common practices, their shortcomings and how these can be addressed to make your Cyber Exposure Management program effective, improve your bottom line, and avoid much of the carnage.

Once you have read this book you will:

- Better understand what a comprehensive cyber exposure management program consists of and its benefit to your bottom line
- Appreciate the compelling need for such a program in your enterprise
- Recognize the ever changing nature of the cyber landscape and the concomitant need for an adaptive, evolving cyber exposure management program
- Understand the difference between cyber risk and cyber exposure, and why it matters.
- Understand the dangers that arise from secondary cyber exposures
- See that technically focused approaches are bound to miss dealing with key exposures
- Conclude that the silos and gaps present in most enterprises need to be addressed and resolved as part of your eCEM program

- Understand the importance of ownership and accountability of cyber exposure elements
- See how the culture of an enterprise is a vital part of any successful cyber exposure management program
- Grasp the importance of metrics and reporting of cyber exposure elements in your enterprise
- Be motivated, and better prepared, to effectively manage your cyber exposures

We begin most chapters with a list of questions that you should be able to answer after you've read that chapter. Scanning this list will allow you to determine the relevance that chapter holds for you.

This book will be continued to be revised in step with the changing cyber exposure environment and experience.

SECTION ONE – Getting your strategy right

It is imperative if you want to effectively manage your cyber exposures to have a strategy that aligns your resources against the threats you face. Sounds simple but is anything but since the threats you face are constantly evolving, are specific to your organization, and not readily apparent. This means package, one size fits all, approaches will not be very effective.

Instead you need to develop a strategy that addresses all of your cyber exposures, maintains your technical defenses and adapts to the ever changing cyber environment. It is my objective in this book to provide you with an approach and basic principles to develop such a strategy.

But remember the cyber eco-system constantly changes so be ready to evolve with it – or suffer the consequences. The choice is yours!

Chapter 1-1 Background

Today the pace of change in malicious cyber events is accelerating. In the past the risks were mainly in someone gaining access to valuable information such as proprietary company information, financial records, customer credit card data, and similar information and then using the information for gain. I am now seeing a rise in harming the ability of an organization, or an individual, to function by disabling key operations, and sometimes demanding a ransom payment to return it to normal. Additionally there is a rise in malicious exposures to harm a company's reputation.

It seems every day a new cyber threat arises, which leads to a great deal of activity to determine how to react to it. This is a strategic mistake. Focusing solely on cyber threats is a losing proposition as there will always be a new cyber threat to deal with, it is technologies version of cyber 'wack-a-mole'. You need to stop playing cyber wack-a-mole and begin to take the offensive against the predators that infest the cyber eco-system we all inhabit.

To accomplish this you need to identify and manage your cyber exposures so you are not always playing catchup. That is not to say you should ignore cyber threats. You need to deal with ones that are prevalent in your cyber eco-system. Rather, you need to also, if you want to get ahead of cyber threats, identify and deal with your organizations cyber exposures. By 'cyber exposures' I mean the vulnerabilities that arise from inhabiting the cyber eco-system. Realize that these vulnerabilities are not just technical but rather are rooted in human behavior, legal and compliance matters, use of social media, the cloud and the Internet of Things (IoT).

A key in improving the likelihood of success in addressing the many cyber exposures your organization faces is understanding the mindset of the members of your organization – the cyber security culture. This can be done by examining attitudes towards cyber exposure, responsibilities towards cyber security, and awareness of the cyber threats in general. In other words how does your organization view cyber security? Is it only a technical concern? Not a real problem? An annoyance to be circumvented? The answers to these and similar questions will go a long way towards understanding the approach you will need to improve your organizations cyber defenses. If your culture treats cyber security poorly then your organization is more likely to undermine your efforts and experience a cyber event.

Chapter 1-2 - A technical problem, isn't it?

What questions will Chapter 1-2 answer for you?

- What exposures are there beyond the technical?
- What am I missing if I only focus on the-technical issues?
- What is the likelihood and potential level of these non technical cyber exposures?
- Why should I care?

By answering the above questions we hope you will better appreciate the need to gain a broad perspective of all the cyber exposures your organization faces.

What cyber exposures are there beyond the technical?

Let us assume for the purposes of this discussion that all your technology is functioning effectively and securely. Do you still have cyber exposures? The answer is a resounding yes! The actual exposures will depend upon the specifics of your organization and its operations. The following list, which is not complete, highlights some key potential exposures:

- Intellectual property issues: Do you use a federally registered trademark in your domain name? Do you use metatags to control your web site positioning and description in search engine results?
- PCI compliance: Have you ensured that all personnel handling credit card transactions mask all but the last four digits when displaying or printing cardholder data?
- Red flag compliance: Are you defined either as a 'financial institution' or a 'creditor'? If the answer is yes have you implemented a red flags identity theft program?
- Social Network Gaffes: Do you monitor all social media sites where you have a presence, or that are used by personnel using your equipment, for posting that may be harmful to your institution?

- Human failures: Do you have a training program that all appropriate staff must attend that focuses on cyber exposures and how to combat them? Do you require all data in transit be encrypted?
- Internet of Things (IoT) exposures. Many devices now have computers embedded in them and communicate for various purposes over the Internet. These can represent an open door to your organization.
- Secondary Cyber Exposures: You need to determine if services and facilities that you rely on, which are managed by others, are addressing their cyber exposures in a manner you find acceptable.

There are many more examples but these should suffice to demonstrate that there is much cyber exposure beyond the technical.

What am I missing if I only focus on the-technical issues?

Clearly you may have a surprise arising from the aforementioned exposures but just as importantly you will not have prepared your organization to respond and minimize the results from such an incident. At a minimum you should review you potential exposures in the following areas:

- Cyber Activity: An overview of all cyber activity across the entire organization, not just in the technology departments. Who accesses what data using what tools and are they secure?
- Privacy: Does a senior level management official currently exist, whose responsibility it is to ensure that personally identifiable information, proprietary institution information, or other sensitive information, is not released, accidentally or intentionally, without the proper authorization and safeguards?

- Computer Systems: Who is responsible to ensure that your computer system(s), networks and other applied cyber technologies are secure?
- Legal: Does your organization and your cloud computer vendor(s), if used, have cyber liability insurance? Have you established intellectual property (IP) or compliance procedures across your entire institution and its many departments and individuals, including each of the following:
  - periodic IP audits accomplished by legal staff or outside counsel, or both
  - training of employees regarding copyright and trademark issues
  - acquisition of all necessary IP rights via licenses, releases or consents
- Security Policies and Procedures: Have you established institution-wide responsibility for records and information management compliance with an experienced records/compliance officer holding a dedicated position?
- Social Media: Does your organization use, or permit management, employees, contactors or vendors to use, any social media platforms, including, but not limited to Facebook, Twitter, foursquare, LinkedIn and MySpace, utilizing equipment furnished by your organization for any purpose?
- Compliance: While you are likely aware of the federal regulations you are subjected to, what are you doing in response to a number of state laws that require you to establish a proactive procedure for determining the severity of a potential data security breach and for providing prompt notification to all individuals who may be adversely affected by such exposures?
- Cloud Computing: Has your institution explored and resolved the following issues with your cloud computing provider:

- whether your institution's data will be stored only in the United States to resolve any jurisdictional issues in the event of a dispute with your provider
- the financial stability of the provider, including reviewing third party audit reports of the provider's security and privacy practices, the results of internal audit reports, a copy of the provider's Disaster Recovery Business Continuity plan and the results of the latest comprehensive test of this plan

- Internet of Things (IoT): Does your organization know of the possible exposures in the following, and if so have you taken steps to secure them?
  - Building Control Systems such as HVAC systems, electrical distribution systems, elevators, or similar systems.
  - Manufacturing or Process control systems such as conveyor lines, machine tools, chemical processes, ovens, and the like.
  - Automated warehousing/distribution systems such as automatic picking conveyor systems, loading and unloading systems, and equipment such as forklifts or similar equipment and systems.
  - Other equipment and devices such as phone systems, office copiers, fax machines, scanners, communication systems, intercoms, or the like.
- Secondary Cyber Exposures: If you found there are services and facilities, managed by others, where you are not comfortable with how they address their cyber exposures have you:

o Notified those parties of your concerns?
o Have they responded in a manner that you are comfortable with?
o If you are uncomfortable with their responses have you looked for alternatives, engaged them in serious further dialog, and otherwise addressed the potential exposures?
o If possible have you gotten insurance against their failure?

What is the likelihood and potential level of these non technical cyber exposures?

- A recent cyber breach report[3] found that the costliest average cause ($168K) was malicious insiders.
- The report[7] also found the mean cost of cyber crime in their survey was $9.5 million, an increase of 21% over the prior year and each compromised data record costs, on average, $214 to fix. Doesn't sound like much until you realize the thefts of records usually are in the tens of thousands of data records range, and sometimes much higher.
- In an older study[4] it was found that 72% of the organizations said they cannot quickly respond to changes in employee access requirements and more than half (52%) cannot keep pace with the number of access changes that come up on a regular basis.
- A settlement of HIPAA claims brought by the Department of Health and Human Services against BlueCross BlueShield of Tennessee ("BCBST") underscores the cost of non-technical exposure. HHS announced on March 13, 2012 that BCBST has agreed to pay $1.5 million to settle claims that

---

[3] HP Enterprises Sponsored 2016 Cost of Data Breach Report conducted by the Ponemon Institute

[4] 2010 Access Governance Trends Survey, Ponemon, April 19, 2010

BCBST violated HIPAA in connection with the theft in 2009 of 57 unencrypted hard drives containing protected health information of over 1 million individuals. The payment to HHS, however, is the tip of the iceberg. According to the Nashville Business Journal, BCBST reported that it has spent nearly $17 million in investigation, notification and protection efforts. Thus, even though privacy class actions typically falter for inability to prove recoverable damages, the BCBST case demonstrates that data breaches can still result in substantial administrative fines and remediation costs.

- Master Card and Visa have removed Global Payments from their approved vendor list as reported in the Wall Street Journal on May 2, 2012.

Why should I care?

Because cyber exposures can impact your bottom line, your reputation, and may even sink your business if you do not pay close attention.

Addressing the technical issues is necessary but not sufficient. You need a comprehensive strategy.

Chapter 1-3 - The problem with Generic solutions

What questions will Chapter 1-3 answer for you?

- Why are industry standards insufficient for your enterprise?

- For a small company isn't it sufficient to keep our anti-virus and anti-malware protections up to date?

- Can I use generic solution as the basis for a program tailored to my enterprise?

Generic describes solutions that are developed from software packages, templates or industry standards such as ISO 27002 mentioned above. Problems arises when templates and standards, that were developed to reflect generalized normative technical exposures, are applied without appreciation of the unique characteristics and requirements of a particular organization. For example, have you heard the statement – 'We are ISO compliant' as though that is a sufficient criterion? Standards are a good technical foundation but for a CEM plan to be effective it must reflect the entire spectrum of cyber exposures the organization faces.

Why are industry standards insufficient for your enterprise?

> ISO itself makes the point: 'This code of practice may be regarded as a starting point for developing organization specific guidelines. Not all of the controls and guidance in this code of practice may be applicable. Furthermore, additional controls and guidelines not included in this standard may be required.'[5]

> Your unique markets, products, procedures, culture, operating and regulatory environments mean that your cyber exposures are unique as well and your plans to address these cyber exposures need to be tailored to your circumstances.

---

[5] ISO/IEC 17799:2000 (E) page xi

What you are really guarding against is the unwarranted assumption that if you implement some magic 'techie' bullet your organization will minimize, if not avoid, cyber exposures. Addressing cyber exposure is going to require constant vigilance especially as you introduce new technologies.

Some questions for you to consider:

- Does your sales force use smart phone and/or tablet computers such as the iPad? If so what company confidential information is contained on them? What access to they have to corporate confidential data?
- Do you use the cloud to store confidential information? Do you allow the staff to use the cloud? How sure are you of your answer?
- Do you use social media, such as Google+, facebook, or Linkedin, to promote your business? In the hiring process?
- Do you provide mobile technology to your employees? If so what security training do they receive?

The above issues are not explicitly addressed in ISO 27002 yet each could represent a significant cyber exposure.

For a small company isn't it sufficient to keep our anti-virus/anti-malware protections up to date?

In a report[6] Symantec found that 18% of all targeted cyber attacks were at organizations with fewer than 250 employees. Why? Because they were easy prey.

---

[6] Internet Security Report 2014 Trends, Symantec April 2014

In a dirrerent survey[7] the respondents were generally satisfied (3+ on a scale of 5) with their security technology even though recent papers[8] take the position that determined attackers can bypass conventional protection at will.

Even small companies have intellectual property, regulatory, compliance, and human issues. Cyber criminals look for easy pickings; 79% of recent hacks[8] were classified as targets of opportunity, i.e. - poor or non-existent protection. So a minimal strategy is not to make it easy for the hacker. Like the old joke you do not have to out run the bear just outrun your companion.

Can I use a generic solution as the basis for a program tailored to my enterprise?

Absolutely. It provides a great starting point. However you need to assess all your cyber exposures to make sure you are allocating your resources where your exposures are.

Some examples of how you might have to tailor your program follow, using the questions posed in the prior paragraph.

Does your sales force use smart phone and/or tablet computers?

If your answer was yes you need to determine the details of your organization's smart phone and tablet usage (i.e., how they are acquired and/or supplied, what information is available on them, what access do they have to corporate date, is the data encrypted or not, are there restrictions on usage and or internet access, etc.).

---

[7] 2014 Computer Crime and Security Survey from the Computer Security Institute

[8] http://www.h-online.com/security/news/item/New-attack-bypasses-anti-virus-software-997621.html

Do you use social media, such as Google+, facebook, or Linkedin, to promote your business? In the hiring process?

> If your answer was yes you need to determine the details of your organization's social media usage (i.e., widespread across all platforms with no access restrictions, restricted to certain platforms, access restricted to certain individuals, etc.). Then use this information to formulate an enforceable social media policy with the input of legal counsel, human resources, and public relations/marketing. Ensure the policy is well promulgated with training as appropriate.

Do you provide mobile technology to your employees? If so what security training do they receive?

> If your answer was yes you need to determine the details of your organization's mobile technology provisioning (what technologies are in use, how are they provided, what guidelines on usage exist, what charges are permitted, etc.).

Then for each area you need to use the information gathered to formulate enforceable appropriate policies and procedures with the input of legal counsel, human resources, and public relations/marketing. Ensure these policies and procedures are well promulgated with training as appropriate. Make sure the policies and procedures are reviewed on a regular basis to make sure they reflect changes that may occur in technology and other areas. Finally make sure the policies and procedures are audited to make sure they are being complied with. If not and you suffer an incident you may find yourselves liable beyond the immediate loss.

Are you aware of the exposures created by the various 'smart devices' at use in your organization?

Sometimes called the Internet of Things (IoT) there is an explosion of devices and equipment that communicates over the Internet. There are many reasons for this which we will not go into. However every device that is using the Internet to communicate represents a door into your organization. Do you know where these 'doors' are? Have you secured them? Do you monitor them?

In summary, generic standards are useful as a starting point but they need to be modified to reflect the specifics of your organization, markets and practices.

SECTION 2 – UNDERSTAND ALL YOUR CYBER EXPOSURES

I believe that it is imperative that you understand, and perform triage on, all of your cyber exposures. Recent history shows the fallacy of focusing cyber defenses on purely technical matters. It is likely defending a properties front door with all types of security yet leaving open doors in the back. Think I am exaggerating? Remember the Sony hack? If not you can read about it at https://en.wikipedia.org/wiki/Sony_Pictures_hack.

Chapter 2-1 – Understanding Cyber Exposure

We will begin by reviewing the nature of Cyber exposure. The following are key characteristics of cyber exposures:

- Constantly evolving and adapting – There was an increase of 23% in the number of new vendors identities exposures[9]
- Ubiquitous – In 2015 Symantec encountered more than 430 million unique variants of malware across the entire range of electronic devices and networks
- Predatory – On May 3, 2012 hackers threatened a Belgian bank they would release customer data unless the bank paid $197,000 within a day[10].
- Vindictive – When the US government shut down Megaupload, Anonymous attacked the US Department of Justice website among others.
- Growing – The Ponemon Institute reported growth of 23% in the cost of cyber attacks from 2014 to 2015.
- Costly – In a recent Ponemon study[11] the average cost of a cyber crime hit $9.5 million last year and cost companies over $200 per compromised data record, according to the Ponemon Institute..
- Multifaceted – While technology is an underlying driver the exposures arise in different areas such as legal, compliance, personnel, intellectual property and operations.
- Acts as a conduit – Provides a path to other exposures

In summary cyber exposure is a very real, growing problem with very real consequences. You ignore it at your peril.

Some of the questions this book will help you answer are:

- ♦ Why is eCEM important for your organization?
- ♦ What are the important components of an eCEM?
- ♦ Why does an eCEM have to be adaptive and evolving?

---

[9] Symantec 2015 Internet security threat report
[10] Computerworld May 3, 2012
[11] Second Annual Cost of Cyber Crime Study August 2014

- Why are generic cyber risk programs insufficient?
- What are the consequences of failing to establish accountability and ownership of the cyber exposures in the enterprise?
- How do I gain buy-in from my stakeholders to assure we are all on the same page regarding cyber exposures?
- What role does organizational culture play in an CEM?
- Why do I need to have metrics to measure the risk aspects of my business?

We hear about major cyber failure on a regular basis. Recent examples include: Yahoo's data hack in late 2016 is expected to cost more than $100 million and may be much more as more than class action suits wend through the courts, FACC, an Australian based aresospace parts manufacturer, loss, in early 2016, of up to 20.4 million. In its most recent (2015) annual report the FBI's Internet Crime Complaint Center received over 288 thousand complaints . These failures cost billions of dollars, plus negative impacts to reputations, growth and stakeholder value. Directors need to understand the broad potential of cyber exposures, so they can independently validate senior executive claims. Senior executives need to understand cyber exposures so they can better manage them. It's time for visionary corporate leaders to implement enterprise risk management programs that work.

Over the last 4 years, we analyzed many of the high-profile cyber management failures and determined that most failures can be traced to the following:

- Viewing cyber exposure as a technical problem: Because technology is at the heart of many of the cyber exposures many believe technology is also the solution. While technology has a significant role to play there are other facets to the exposures such as legal, personnel, physical, operational and regulation that must be addressed.
- Generic solutions: Because cyber exposure is viewed as a technology issue, many organizations believe that all they need do is install a technology

solution – such as Norton, McAfee, Bitdefender or Kapersky - and their cyber exposure will be managed.

- Delegating down: Because cyber exposures are new, most senior executives are uncomfortable addressing them and are much more comfortable delegating them to their technology department.
- Undisciplined: 79% of the victims were targets of opportunity who fell prey because they were found to possess an (often easily) exploitable weakness[12]

The following pages will discuss cyber exposures vs. cyber threats. Following that we will describe the steps you can take to effectively manage your cyber exposures.

---

[12] Verizon 2014 Data BREACH Investigations Report

Chapter 2-2 – Know all your Cyber Exposures

If you don't know where you are going, you will wind up somewhere else

Yogi Berra

The questions Chapter 2-2 will answer follow:

- How do we recognize the full range of our vulnerability to cyber exposures?
- Where should the effort report?
- What level should be responsible for CEM?
- How do we prioritize our efforts? (risk appetite)

We have seen in previous chapters the issues that arise when the focus of a CEM program is purely technical. We will now explore alternatives through responding to the questions.

How do we recognize the full range of our vulnerability to cyber exposures?

Given the broad range of cyber exposures the first step is to get a strategic overview assessment of yours. We call it a strategic overview since you will be attempting to determine where your exposures lie and the potential magnitude. Without this as a starting point how can you set priorities and allocate resources in an intelligent manner?

One approach it to create a task force consisting of representatives from your technical staff, corporate auditor, general counsel, lines of business representatives and Human Relations and task them to discuss and create a list of your organizations possible cyber exposures with an estimate of high/medium/low impact.

An alternative approach is to have an outside expert conduct a strategic level cyber exposure review. This can be done with minimal impact on your organization and will provide you with the strategic overview of your cyber exposures to allow the determination of priorities and to allocate resources accordingly.

While every organization will have some unique exposures the following list provides a general guide that covers the majority of cyber exposures:

- Cyber Activity – A general review of the types of cyber activity present within your organization.

- Privacy – An inventory of the types of information you create, store and process. What is confidential, what is privileged, etc.

- Computer Systems – What technologies you use and how you manage and control them.

- Legal – What legal exposures you have regarding your use of technology and how you protect your intellectual property.

- Security Policies and Procedures – What security policies and procedures you have in place, how they are managed, audited and updated to assure effectiveness.

- Social Media – How you use, or allow your staff to use, social media when at work.

- Compliance – What regulations concerning technology you are affected by and what efforts to you have in place to comply.

- Cloud Computing – Inventory your use of cloud computing, the contracts you use the services under, and what protections you have in place?

- Internet of Things – You need to know what devices and equipment are in use within your organization that communicate over the Internet and how secure they are.

- Secondary Cyber Exposure – These are the cyber exposure that arise from services or business partners that you rely on and that are not as diligent in their security practices as you would wish.

Where should the effort report?

For reasons stated earlier it is imperative that the effort be seen to have support at the highest level. It should provide reports to the board of directors through a designated C level executive.

What level should be responsible for CEM?

Ultimately the management of risk, of which cyber exposures are a significant part, is the responsibility of the board and CEO. They can designate a function to provide them with the required information but they are the ones who will be held responsible should an cyber event occur.

 A good place to start is your current Enterprise Risk Management program. A CEM program can be a part of a larger ERM but cyber exposures have unique aspects that mean they should have a dedicated focus.

How do we prioritize our efforts? (risk appetite)

Once you have uncovered all of your cyber exposures and have a rough idea of their criticality you can integrate them into your existing risk appetite program or you can treat the cyber exposures separately using the strategic cyber exposure review mentioned above as a starting point.

If you follow the above steps you are well on your way to creating an effective Cyber Exposure Management program (eCEM©).

Chapter 2-3 - Cyber Exposure vs. Cyber Threats

What questions will Chapter 2-3 answer for you?
- What is the difference between cyber threats and cyber exposures
- Why is this important
- What steps should you consider in order to address you cyber exposures.

We hear a great deal about rising cyber threats. It seems every day a new cyber threat arises, which leads to a great deal of activity to determine how to react to it. This is a strategic mistake. Focusing solely on cyber threats is a losing proposition as there will always be a new cyber threat to deal with, it is technologies version of cyber 'wack-a-mole'. You need to stop playing cyber wack-a-mole and begin to take the offensive against the predators that infest the cyber eco-system we all inhabit.

Instead what you need to do is to identify and manage your cyber exposures so you are not always playing catchup. That is not to say you should ignore cyber threats. You need to deal with ones that are prevalent in your cyber eco-system. Rather, you need to also, if you want to get ahead of cyber threats, identify and deal with your organizations cyber exposures. By 'cyber exposures' we mean the vulnerabilities that arise from inhabiting the cyber eco-system. You need not be doing anything exotic or leading edge just use computers, smart devices, networks and the Internet and you are in a cyber eco-system that has predators hunting for vulnerabilities. Realize that these vulnerabilities are not just technical but rather are rooted in human behavior, legal and compliance matters, use of social media, the cloud and the Internet of Things (IoT).

In order to help you address your cyber exposure you should consider approaching from two perspectives.

1. You need to understand the mindset of the members of your organization. This can be done by examining attitudes towards cyber exposure, responsibilities towards cyber security, and awareness of the cyber threats in general. In other

words how does your organizations culture view cyber security? Is it only a technical concern? Not a real problem? An annoyance to be circumvented? The answers to these and similar questions will go a long way towards understanding the approach you will need to improve your organizations cyber defenses. If your culture treats cyber security poorly then your organization is more likely to experience a cyber event.

2. You need to identify as near as possible all your cyber exposures. You need to know if you have major cyber exposures and so that you can begin to prioritize and address them. If you are not aware of all your cyber exposures then you will be defending your organization from the known threats while leaving major access paths into your organization for predators to exploit. And the predators are like most people, they will go for the easy prey.

With this information in hand you have the foundation to create an effective Cyber Exposure Management Program specifically for your organization. One that address your exposures and sets you on a proactive cyber defense path.

Chapter 2-4 - Secondary Cyber Exposure

Virtually all cyber exposure programs today are directed at addressing the cyber exposures an organization faces from its own resources and activities and from outside sources. This is necessary but not sufficient.

Why? Because most organizations also face secondary cyber exposures that they are neither aware of nor prepared to address. For example, many organizations do not manage, or own their own properties but inhabit facility space managed by someone else. That someone, generally a building manager, is responsible for facilitating building services (HVAC, elevators, water, sewage, electricity, and the like). Most of these building managers are investing heavily in various devices and systems, under the common category of the Internet of Things commonly called IoT, to allow them to be more effective managers. All with an eye to improve their costs and provide improved performance to their clients. Unfortunately if the building managers do not pay attention to their building's cyber exposures inherent in IoT, the buildings will become targets of cyber predators. The implication of this is that if such an attack occurs the occupants of their facilities will suffer a disruption that they were unaware was even possible and for which they are unprepared.

So what should you do? The following are some suggested steps

1. Identify where you might have secondary cyber exposures by determining.
    a. Who manages your facilities
    b. What external services you are dependent upon
    c. If your business partners[i] have cyber exposure management programs. Try to determine if they are effective. You might consider asking them to take our cyber exposure toolkit available at the global risk academy
    https://globalriskacademy.com/p/cyb er-toolkit. It would provide you with a

quick assessment of a building's cyber exposure program.
   d. If there are dependencies that are not directly under your control.
2. Determine the potential impact of your secondary cyber exposures
   a. Consider triage to categorize and prioritize your secondary cyber exposures:
      i. critical secondary exposures – those which, if an event occurred, would materially affect your organization,
      ii. moderate secondary exposures – those which would affect your organization but not materially,
      iii. modest secondary exposures – those which would only affect minor aspects of you organizations operation,
      iv. nominal secondary exposure – those which even if , even if a cyber event occurred, the impact on your organization would be minimal.
   b. Determine what is the effectiveness of your facilities cyber exposure management programs. Once again you might consider asking them to take our cyber exposure toolkit available at the global risk academy https://globalriskacademy.com/p/cyber-toolkit. It would provide you with a quick assessment of their cyber exposure program.
3. Take appropriate steps to address these secondary cyber exposures.
   a. Work with business partners to improve your protection against cyber exposure
   b. Get appropriate cyber insurance
   c. Change organization to minimize secondary exposures. Consider alternatives.
   d. Ensure you have the necessary legal protections by way of contractual agreements including liability and indemnification provisions.

If you want to have a secure cyber eco-system you need to care about your secondary cyber exposures and have a program underway to address them, or suffer when the unexpected occurs.

SECTION 3 – MANAGING YOUR EFFORTS

In this section we will provide some guidance, suggestions and strategies for your consideration in managing your cyber exposures. As we have often said every organizations is different so you need to use, and modify, this material in a manner that make it useful to your situation.

Chapter 3-1 - Existing Cyber Security Efforts

We assume you have a cyber security program in place. If you do not have an existing cyber security program stop reading and develop and implement such a program. Once you have one in place then come back and continue.

For an existing cyber security program we strongly recommend you make sure your program includes the following:

- Written cyber security policies and regulations that you publish and distribute to all employees, vendors and contractors.
- Education regarding your cyber security policies and regulations that is required of all members of your organization, including senior executives, vendors and contractors.
- Making sure all default settings and vendor supplied passwords have been changed from those initially supplied.
- Sensitive information[13] that you handle, process or store is identified, responsible party identified, protected by encryption and access controls? Are they monitored?
- Backup copies for all organizational data, especially sensitive data, made on a regular basis with off-site, secured storage.
- Do your disaster recovery/business continuity plans (DR/BCP) include sections covering your cyber eco system, its many components, it recovery and continuing operation should an unforeseen event occur.
- Your normal operating procedures should include change management and configuration management processes. The detail documentation should include who is responsible and how that individual will be monitored and managed.

---

[13] Sensitive information includes but is not limited to personal identifiable information, proprietary organizational information, and other sensitive information.

- Firewalls that cover outbound transmissions as well as inbound.
- Wiping clean all devices and materials disposed of. This includes copiers, printers, cell phone, other intelligent devices as well as the usual hard drives, pc's and laptops.
- Both physical and electronic intrusion detection and monitoring.
- BYOD policies and procedures

This list is not meant to be exhaustive, rather indicative of the details that your existing cyber security plans should include. To assure a high level of confidence in your cyber security plans and programs we recommend you have an outside expert conduct a review to uncover any deficiencies.

Chapter 3-2 - Strategic Segmentation

The following list provides thoughts on tasks and actions that can be pursued individually if a full scale program is not a viable option at this time. The order they are presented in does not reflect importance as what is the most important will be the ones that benefit your organization the most and only you can determine segment priority.

Internet of Things (IoT)

The Internet of Things (IoT) consists of all the intelligent devices and systems that are connected to your network and thence to the Internet. They can represent a wide open door into your organization if not secured.

The problem arises in that many of the devices have minimal security and are installed using default settings, which are known to the bad guys out there. And in many cases the installations occurred with no coordination with IT or security functions, as they are, other than the network connection, independent devices paid for and used by business functions for managing their specific function. And in many cases needed only the approval of their management chain, so no one else knows they are there.

Some of the places IoT devices may reside are building control systems (HVAC, UPS, electrical distribution, lighting systems, elevators, or similar systems.), process control systems (manufacturing lines, machine tools, chemical processes, ovens, and the like), automated warehousing/distribution systems (automated picking conveyor systems, loading and unloading systems and equipment such as forklifts, or similar systems), intelligent equipment or devices (such as phone systems, office copiers, fax machines, scanners, communication systems, intercoms, or like devices), and building services including those that process maintenance requests and tracking, managing building control systems, scheduling building resources, managing visitor traffic, or the like.

For each IoT device found you need to inventory the specifics, including the responsible party, determine what security, if any are in use, make sure the operation is monitored, audited and tested on a regular basis to assure safe and secure operation.

Cyber Security Culture

A key to successfully addressing the many cyber exposures your organization faces is understanding the mindset of the members of your organization – the cyber security culture. This can be done by examining attitudes towards cyber exposure, responsibilities towards cyber security, and awareness of the cyber threats in general. In other words how does your organization view cyber security? Is it only a technical concern? Not a real problem? An annoyance to be circumvented? The answers to these and similar questions will go a long way towards understanding the approach you take to improve your organizations cyber defenses. If your culture treats cyber security poorly then your organization is much more likely to experience a cyber event.

You may wish to consult with experts in the field of culture management, or we have included a link to our Cyber Security Culture Barometer which is free, and can provide some initial guidance.

In summary: cyber security culture matters and cyber security culture can be managed.

Regulatory Environment

You need to, with the guidance and advice of a trusted legal advisor, review your cyber operations to make sure you are in compliance with all the regulations that apply to your organization. This is not a simple task since many jurisdictions have unique regulations that may apply and if you have a presence on the Internet you may inadvertently be operating within jurisdictions and not know of it.

In addition you need to make sure you are in compliance with supra national regulations that may apply should you process credit cards. Specifically the Payment Card Data Security Industry Standard (PCI DSS). Others may apply which is why you need to enlist a trusted legal advisor to determine what applies.

Cloud Computing

Use of cloud services for data storage and processing is growing and brings cost benefits which can lead to entry into agreements that do not reflect the necessary security and other protections. First you need to determine if any such agreements are in place in your organization and then make sure they consider the following.

Whether your organization's data will be stored only in your home jurisdiction to resolve any jurisdictional issues in the event of a dispute with your provider; and the financial stability of the provider, including reviewing third party audit reports of the provider's security and privacy practices, a copy of their cyber liability insurance, the results of internal audit reports, a copy of the provider's Disaster Recovery/Business Continuity plan and the results of the latest comprehensive test of this plan.

The following items should be discussed in any contract you agree to:

- where your transactions and data will be stored and how you can remove them, and at what cost
- how the removal of your company's transactions and data may be moved from the provider, including the security and cost of such a move;
- what kind of security safeguards will the provider apply to your transactions and data
- what terms of limits of liability is the provider imposing on the transaction
- who will control breach incident response and bear the cost
- whether the provider will indemnify the organization and, if so, under what circumstances

You need to also find out whether your cloud provider does the following:

- conducts network penetration tests of its cloud service infrastructure regularly as prescribed by industry best practices
- Segment and recover transactions and data for a specific customer in the case of a failure or data loss
- Sanitizes all computing resources of your transactions and data once you have ended the arrangement
- Provide documentation that sets out the process and rationale for moving transactions and data from one physical location to another
- encrypts transactions and data at rest within its environment, and that in transit
- has anti-malware programs installed on all systems that support the cloud service offerings?
- maintain logs for traffic monitoring and auditing including who accessed your account, what they accessed and how long they were logged in

Privacy

There are several keys to addressing cyber exposures arising from privacy concerns. They are:

- Identifying all the sensitive information[14] that resides in, or is processed by your cyber eco-system along with the responsible party for that information.
- Making sure such sensitive information is secure, monitored and audited at all times.
- Making sure such sensitive information does not leave your facilities unless secured and a responsible party identified. This includes staff intelligent devices used for work purposes, the disposal of equipment, and off site storage.

Education & Communication

Key is that you have a set of cyber security policies and procedures that you distribute throughout the organization. It is important that you have programs in place that educate all personnel not only in these policies and procedures but why they exist, the rationale behind needing cyber security and its importance.

This also needs to apply to all levels of the organization.

This education should occur on an ongoing basis since the cyber threats you face and the cyber exposures that exist will continue to evolve as the predators create new was to disrupt your operations, new technologies arise, and you and your business partners change your business practices and procedures.

You also should consider having an internet accessible site that has your cyber security policies, procedures, and best practices available. You might also consider having a newsletter that updates all staff on new threats, practices and other cyber security considerations.

---

[14] Sensitive information includes but is not limited to personal identifiable information, proprietary organizational information, and other sensitive information.

Ransomware

First some ransomware history. The first known malware extortion attack, the "AIDS Trojan" was written by Joseph Popp in 1989. Had design failure but did rip off some individuals. Public Key Cryptography first noted was in IEEE paper by A,M. Yung in 1996 entitled *Cryptovirology: extortion-based security threats and countermeasures. Presented at the IEEE Symposium on Security and Privacy.* Ransomware began to get really noticed in August 2012 by the US FBI (*New Internet scam: Ransomware)* In 2012, a major ransomware Trojan known as Reveton began to spread followed by Encrypting ransomware reappeared in September 2013 with a Trojan known as *CryptoLocker.*

More recently Petya was first discovered in March 2016; unlike other forms of encrypting ransomware, the malware aimed to infect the master boot record, installing a payload which encrypts the file tables of the NTFS file system the next time that the infected system boots, blocking the system from booting into Windows at all until the ransom is paid.

In May 2017, the WannaCry ransomware attack spread through the Internet, using an exploit vector named EternalBlue, which was leaked from the U.S. National Security Agency. The ransomware attack, unprecedented in scale, infected more than 230,000 computers in over 150 countries, using 20 different languages to demand money from users using Bitcoin cryptocurrency. WannaCrypt demanded US$300 per computer.

On October 24, 2017, some users in Russia and Ukraine reported a new ransomware attack, named "Bad Rabbit", which follows a similar pattern to WannaCry and Petya by encrypting the user's file tables and then demands a BitCoin payment to decrypt them

The General way Ransomware operates it does not require administrative privileges like other malware. Instead, it relies and preys on the permissions a victim user has on their assigned computer and within an organization, to encrypt the files that the specific user has access to, either locally on their own computer and/or across the organization's network on corporate file share servers.

The three most common ways it gets into a cyber eco-system are:

1. Infected email attachment
2. Embedded Macros in Documents
3. Security lapses (poor patch policies and execution, poor web filtering, weak antivirus and endpoint protection, allowing executables entry via email.)

There are three aspects you need to consider in order to protect your organization.

1. Technical – Maintain firewalls and antivirus, scan/strip executables from email (including zipped files), Increase DNS visibility, consider implementing sinkhole and web filtering capabilities, perform backups on strict schedule (daily?), enforce least privilege authority, consider disabling Flash and windows scripting host
2. Cultural – staff education, secure cyber exposures – both primary and secondary
3. Actions –Create a response plan; have drills to clean up environment and reload backups.

Detecting a ransomware event is unfortunately reasonably simple. First when attempting to access network you find shared files are encrypted. Means the server is likely compromised. Second, if a local user finds local file is now encrypted. That machine is likely compromised and needs be immediately isolated. Third you get a pop up message with ransom notice

Should you find yourself in a ransomware event use your response plan. what elements are infected? What equipment, devices? Can you isolate them. How did you get infected? What backups are available? What is time frame for correction? What do you tell your customers? Business partners? Then identify infected devices, disconnect, perform shut down and cleanse, finally reload backups.

If you have no response plan are are taken by surprise there are some questions you need to quickly answer. Do you have clean backups? How quickly can you get them? Can you clean up your environment and restart? Can you get a replacement environment and restart? Do you have time to have an expert perform a forensic examination? Paying the ransom – Assume you have exhausted all other avenues, realize you may be entrapped and have to pay again in future

There are some additiona considerations such as outside services that will assist in recovery and repair. And make sure you do proper backups and install protection, and educate staff in proper security behavior.

Chapter 3-3 - Managing Cyber Exposures (vs cyber risks)

We hear a great deal about rising cyber threats. It seems every day a new cyber threat arises, which leads to a great deal of activity to determine how to react to it. This is a strategic mistake. Focusing solely on cyber threats is a losing proposition as there will always be a new cyber threat to deal with, it is technologies version of cyber 'wack-a-mole'. You need to stop playing cyber wack-a-mole and begin to take the offensive against the predators that infest the cyber eco-system we all inhabit.

Instead what you need to do is to identify and manage your cyber exposures so you are not always playing catchup. That is not to say you should ignore cyber threats. You need to deal with ones that are prevalent in your cyber eco-system. Rather, you need to also, if you want to get ahead of cyber threats, identify and deal with your organizations cyber exposures. By 'cyber exposures' we mean the vulnerabilities that arise from inhabiting the cyber eco-system. You need not be doing anything exotic or leading edge just use computers, smart devices, networks and the Internet and you are in a cyber eco-system that has predators hunting for vulnerabilities. Realize that these vulnerabilities are not just technical but rather are rooted in human behavior, legal and compliance matters, use of social media, the cloud and the Internet of Things (IoT).

You need to identify as near as possible all your cyber exposures. You need to know if you have major cyber exposures and so that you can begin to prioritize and address them. If you are not aware of all your cyber exposures then you will be defending your organization from the known threats while leaving major access paths into your organization for predators to exploit. And the predators are like most people, they will go for the easy prey.

To accomplish this you need to understand how to identify your cyber exposures and then understand how best to manage those the you have found. We suggest that to do this, if you do not have the current knowledge and ability, you can either take our course, 'Managing Cyber Exposures' available on the Global Risk Academy (see the links section for the URL) or consult an outside expert.

Chapter 3-4 - Sizing Considerations

There are serious considerations in how small, medium and large organizations address their cyber risks and exposures. The comments below are general guidelines and must be considered in light of your specific organizations structure and culture.

Small organizations

By definition you do not have extensive resources to devote to cyber threats and must rely on people wearing multiple hats. The good news is that many of the suggestions will be easy to implement since you will have fewer exposures and items to deal with. You also should not have major culture or communication issues since there are few of you and you are all in constant and close communication.

While each organization is different we suggest you focus on the simple easy tasks at first. For example making sure all default settings and passwords on your equipment are changed. Also make sure all people in your organization are made aware of the ways predators will try and compromise your organization. This may be done in a small organization by circulating articles and other publications.

Medium organizations

Your size puts you in a difficult situation. You likely have information and assets that the predators covet. Yet your resources are constrained.

This means our strategic segmentation approach may be your best bet. Your specific situation will determine what segments should have priority. As a first step we suggest a communication and education program be established, if possible piggybacked on existing programs, to make sure all in your organization are made aware of the risks that cyber threats pose and the security necessary to stop them.

Large organizations

Likely you have resources to address the issues involved so that means your biggest issues are likely to be in the culture and exposure areas since your size implies a great many access points and personnel with their own agendas.

While each organization is different we suggest you focus on the understanding your organizations culture and exposures as a parallel effort and make sure your existing cyber security personnel are part of the program. An education program that makes sure all in your organization are aware of the ways predators will try and compromise your organization. if such an education program is not already in existence one should be implemented as soon as possible. .

Chapter 3-5 - What is to be done?

For a Cyber Exposure Management program to be effective it needs to be:

- <u>Strategically Broad</u> – Your CEM program needs to be account for all the cyber exposures that exist within and without your organization as well as the cyber exposures that are present in the various relationships and environments that the organization operates within.

- <u>Acculturized</u>[15] – The CEM program needs to reflect, understand, leverage, work within and modify as necessary, the culture of the organization. The mindset must be "we will actively and constantly identify and manage the cyber exposures in our enterprise".

- <u>Adaptive</u> – The program needs to be in synch with, or a step ahead of changes that occur in the organization, risks, markets, technology, regulatory environment and society.

- <u>Metric Based</u> – The CEM program needs measures that reflect the various risks and are part of the organization's standard goals, objectives, and reporting process

Each of these will be expanded upon in the following sections. For an CEM to be effective it <u>must</u> have <u>all</u> of these characteristics.

---

[15] To cause the adoption of a culture, in this case cyber exposure management, throughout the organization.

Chapter 3-6 – Cyber Security Culture Matters

"When I started at IBM I thought culture was important; when I finished I realized that it was the only thing that was important."

> Lew Gerstner from *Who Says Elephants Can't Dance.*

This chapter examines the importance of cyber security culture in an organization and how to make your organizations cyber security culture support your CEM.

What questions will this chapter address?

- What is an organization's cyber security culture?
- Why does cyber security culture matter?
- How can I measure cyber security culture?
- How can I manage cyber security culture?
- How can I improve my results and achieve my objectives by managing the cyber security culture of my organization?

For a cyber exposure management program to be effective it, must become part of the organizations overall culture. This means it must become part of the specific values, beliefs and objectives of the organization and be communicated throughout the organization.

Let us begin by defining what we mean by culture:

> 'Culture' is the set of core values that are held in common across the organization.

You need to understand several points.

- An effective culture cannot incorporate an extensive laundry list. There should be no more than 10 tenets and they should be accepted across the organization.
- Some examples of values are:
  - Ethics
  - Tradition and conformity
  - Rewards
  - Avoidance, or acceptance of risk
- To be effectively managed the culture needs to be measured.

- 'Artifacts' of management approaches are not culture. For example, the difference between top down vs. independent silos is not culture. Other examples of artifacts are: matrix management, mentoring, "Artifacts" is the term introduced by the eminent M.I.T. social psychologist Edgar H. Schein in his landmark writings[16] on organizational culture and leadership. These are the core business activities, management processes, and philosophies that characterize how a company does business on a day-to-day basis. Artifacts can be considered the "things" that are done in the cultural characterization, "how we do things around here." They are a combination of factors common to all organizations and unique to your specific organization.

How to begin. The following are steps to consider.

1- Make sure that the importance of cyber security and its impact is accepted at the highest levels of the organization. This may require an education process including examples of how your organizations cyber security has helped or hindered the achievement of significant objectives. You will need a champion at the highest level to succeed.

2- Determine if your organization has a functioning cyber security culture. This is not a trivial exercise since, in many cases the cyber security culture has not been formalized, and, if it has, it too often confuses the artifacts mentioned above with the values. You are looking to see if there is one set of standards and beliefs that the vast majority of the organization supports, or are there different sets of cyber security beliefs and values depending upon one's level in the organization, or in different silos? There are many techniques to determine the situation. The easiest is to survey a

---

[16] Organization Culture and Leadership (1985) ISBN 1-55542-487-2

representative sample of the organization to see what cyber security beliefs and values are held.

3- If yes, formalize the cyber security values and create measures to manage them. The first step is to document the shared cyber security values. If they have not already been written down, then determine the various levels of maturity for each. For example, if the value is that we are going to use cyber security measures everyone can understand the range of maturity stages might include:

   a. Level 1 – cyber security measures are not understood and are rarely discussed at serious business meetings

   b. Level 2 – cyber security measures are mentioned but with little conviction and without response that can be seen

   c. Level 3 – cyber security measures are in place but largely looking backward. There are responses but rarely targeted with unpredictable results.

   d. Level 4 – cyber security measures are clear and generally understood. Cyber security is moving toward being more predictive than reactive

   e. Level 5 – cyber security measures look forward, are positive, and are understood and valued because they include everything that is important.

4- If no or unsure, survey the organization to determine what, if any cyber security values exist, are shared, and their commonality. Then, depending upon on what is found:

   a. Determine the attributes of cyber security excellence for your organization. When engaged in this task remember that the attributes of cyber security excellence need to be understood and appreciated by all levels of the organization to be effective. It is generally helpful when conducting this exercise to engage an experienced practitioner who understands values and culture.

b. Determine the values that predict acquisition of these attributes. For example if the attribute is to operate secure systems with the minimal performance impact, the values that support this attribute might include:

   i. To view cyber security as part of the whole
   ii. To recognize there is no end to improving cyber security
   iii. To use a yardstick everyone can read
   iv. To be guided by logic not emotion

c. Use these cyber security values to construct a set of measures as outlined in step 2 above.

d. Collect data and report on the integration and maturity of the values. To do this requires the establishment of cyber security measures for each, then determining the level through data collection and reporting the results, not only to upper management but throughout the organization.

e. Use reports to manage the culture within your organization. That is to increase the acceptance of the values that will help you achieve the excellence you previously defined.

This approach provides a framework allowing your organization to adopt the cyber security values necessary for success, diagnose opportunities for improvement, and prescribe remedies.

This is not a one size fits all solution, as each organization will have different attributes of excellence and cyber security values. However, it is our experience that there are some cyber security values that seem remarkably constant, such as how cyber security decisions are made. Further it is our experience that in a successful organization cyber security values remain the same across the shop floor, cubicle farm, or executive suite.

Human performance has everything to do with the cyber security culture within which an individual functions. If the cyber security culture is right – and compatible with the individual's values – his/her performance will be optimized. So, in order to maximize human performance, you need to define your cyber security culture, measure your cyber security culture and manage your cyber security culture to align with your objectives.

In summary: cyber security culture matters, cyber security culture can be measured, and cyber security culture can be managed.

Chapter 3-7 - Delegating Down

What questions will Chapter 3-7 answer for you?

- What problems can arise if pushed down the technical hierarchy?
- What problems can arise if pushed down into the lines of business or other hierarchy?

This issue arises because many C-level executives are not knowledgeable in technology and as a result are uncomfortable dealing directly with cyber exposures. Their style is to delegate, which unfortunately can lead to difficulties in this area.

What problems can arise if pushed down the technical hierarchy?

People deal with what they know and the technical hierarchy knows technology so they will focus on the technical issues.

How would you address the following questions, which are only a small sample, if your organization's cyber exposure was delegated to the technical hierarchy?

- What is our intellectual property exposure on the web?
- How compliant are we with the State laws regarding privacy breaches?
- What training for staff on cyber exposures is needed? How is it funded? Who provides it?
- Who would identify cyber exposures in the lines of business?
- Who writes and distributes organization wide related policies?
- Who acquires cyber liability insurance? How do they determine cyber exposures?
- Who verifies that your trademarks are properly protected on your web, or in other electronic communications?
- Who is responsible to track and deal with complaints or claims alleging invasions of or injury to privacy, identity theft, theft of

information, breach of information security, software copyright infringement or content infringement?

In summary the technical exposures get good attention but the non-technical cyber exposures are usually not addressed.

What problems can arise if pushed down into the line of business, or other, hierarchy?

As stated previously people deal with what they know and the line of business hierarchy knows business issues so they will focus on these and only address the technical issues as they relate to their line of business.

If cyber risk is relegated to the lines of business how would you address the following questions?

Some questions are the same:

- What is our intellectual property exposure on the web?
- How compliant are we with the State laws regarding privacy breaches?
- What training for staff on cyber exposures is needed? How is it funded? Who provides it?
- Who acquires cyber liability insurance? How do they determine cyber exposures?
- Who verifies that your trademarks are properly protected on your web, or in other electronic communications?
- Who is responsible to track and deal with complaints or claims alleging invasions of or injury to privacy, identity theft, theft of information, breach of information security, software copyright infringement or content infringement?

And some are different.

- Who publishes and distributes written computer and information system security policies and procedures to the employees?

If each line of business does its own, who finds and resolves differences?

- Who monitors, restricts or prohibits employees, vendors and contractors access to company information?
- Who monitors and controls web access?
- Who monitors and disciplines cyber policies and procedures required for a secure environment?
- Who resolves the cross business unit, or silo, issues?

There are just a few of the issues that must be resolved when responsibility for cyber exposures and security is delegated.

If the responsibilities are diffused throughout the organization then how are the following addressed?

- Who has responsibility to bring exposures, real and potential, to the attention of the board? C level executives? If not explicit how does it get done?
- How will cyber exposures be reported on a regular basis?
- How will resources to address cyber exposures and incidents be requested and allocated?
- How will cyber exposure awareness be raised? And by whom?

These questions should raise your awareness of the issues that arise when the responsibility for addressing cyber exposures is delegated. Much activity can, and should be delegated with specific assignments. However, every organization needs to have and understand a basic cyber exposure strategy. In the following chapters we provide our thoughts on several approaches that have proven successful.

Chapter 3-8 - Discipline? What discipline?

The questions Chapter 3-8 will answer for you.

- Are you sure your confidential information (corp. strategies, client private info, banking, etc.) is secure?
- Why it matters that your passwords are secure.
- Is encryption too much hassle?
- Does it matter how we dispose of confidential information? Old computers? Old disk drives?
- Does it matter that we allow staff access to full internet? Social media sites?
- What is the down side of cloud computing?
- How are new technologies integrated, absorbed and understood?

Before we begin to answer these questions we need to define what we mean by discipline. Discipline, in this regard, is the likelihood that your employees will understand and follow your policies and procedures regarding cyber exposures.

We raise this point because of a recent survey wherein 59% of companies surveyed did not have, or did not strictly enforce, access policies and 61% did not immediately check access requests against security policies before granting access[17].

If you do not have such policies and procedures you have a much larger problem regarding your organization's cyber exposures. We suggest you create and develop them. If you are unsure how to do so we suggest you take our courses on Advanced Cyber Exposure Management (parts 1 and 2) at the Global Risk Academy the URL's are:
http://globalriskacademy.com/p/cyber-exposure1
http://globalriskacademy.com/p/cyber-exposure2

To better understand why discipline is important consider the following.

---

[17] 2010 Access Governance Trends Survey, Ponemon, April 19, 2010

Are you sure your confidential information (corp. strategies, client private info, banking, etc.) is secure?

Consider the following statistics taken from the 2016 Data Breach Investigations Report from Verizon.

- 77% of breaches had insider participation.
- 13% of people tested click on a phising attachment.
- 63% of confirmed data breaches involved weak, default or stolen passwords.

Clearly organizations are more vulnerable than they think.

Why it matters that your passwords are secure.

If they are not secure, or if they are easily guessable, such as 'Password" then you have no security. You are then considered a target of opportunity.

If you do not think this is a problem you need to consider this: in a recent breach 32 million passwords were taken from Rockyou, a company that makes software for users of social media sites such as Facebook. An analysis of the passwords found that 1% of the people used 123456 as their password and 20% of the people used from a pool of 5,000 passwords[18].

Lincoln National mistakenly printed a user name and password on its web site and allowed employees and affiliates to share usernames and passwords allowing unauthorized access to 1.2 million customers.

Is encryption too much hassle?

---

[18] 'If your password is 123456, just make it hack me', New York Times, January 21, 2010

Encryption brings to mind complex schemes and in depth mathematical knowledge. This is not true. All that is needed today is to make sure you check the SSL box when setting up your email and password protecting documents in the options box. Virtually every major offering allows protection of your documents and transmittals. If you do not use the option you are opening the door to the hackers.

- AvMed Health plans reported two laptops stolen. One had encrypted data and no harm was done. The other was unprotected allowing access to 1.2 million patient accounts.

Does it matter how we dispose of confidential information? Old computers? Old disk drives? Copiers?

The answer is a resounding yes. All media needs to be destroyed or treated so that your data is no longer accessible. There are standards such as the Department of Defense 5520.22M (NISPOM) for hard drives. If you do not think this is important consider the following incidents:

- Affinity Health Plans had lost 409,000 records because they disposed of a digital copier without wiping the copier's hard drive.

- South Shore hospital lost 800,000 patient records because the tapes containing the data were not destroyed but deployed to an affiliate.

There are many more examples. The net is destroy the data totally or it may come back to harm you.

Does it matter that we allow staff access to full internet? Social media sites?

Historically there are studies showing that 50 percent of employees use their work computers for personal use. (45% send personal emails, 33% read the daily news, 31% investigate travel, etc.)

Websense did a study several years ago that came up with the figure of personal Internet usage while at work, of over 5.9 hours per week.

If you really want to see the dark side Google 'social media misuse examples'. I found over 3 million entries in under .17 seconds.

You want some examples:

- 67% of respondents already use their own mobile devices for work (CBS Money Watch)
- 80% of all BYOD usage is completely unmanaged – SecureEdge Network
- 77% pf employees have received no instructions regarding BYOD usage- All things digital

What is the down side of cloud computing?

Megaupload was at one time the largest file sharing (cloud based) service. They had over 150 million registered users including many legitimate organizations storing very large files on their site. Unfortunately for these organizations, when the government shut down Megaupload they shut down and took away the servers and these files were no longer available. By some estimates over 10,000 legitimate businesses have taken a severe hit because of the lost access to these files and the information they contained.

How are new technologies integrated, absorbed and understood?

Tablets, such as the iPad, are proliferating in many organizations without any understanding of the exposure they bring. With 8 gigabytes of storage there is a lot of information that might be contained. Here are some questions you should ask regarding their usage:

- Do you have a set of standards for the use of such devices?
- Does it include making sure there is password protection?

- Company confidential data, if loaded, is encrypted?
- If the device is company supplied is personal use allowed?
- Are there restrictions on Internet usage, and/or sites?

Caution is necessary.

The bottom line is that without structure and disciplined adherence to strong policies and procedures it is likely potential cyber exposures will cause harm to your bottom line and reputation.

Chapter 3-9 – Adaptive

'It is not the strongest of the species that survives, nor the most intelligent, but the one that is most responsive to change'

Charles Darwin

In this chapter we will set out what you will have to do to make your organizations cyber exposure management (CEM) program adaptive. You will understand:

- Why it is it important to develop an adaptive CEM.
- What are the characteristics of an adaptive CEM?
- How you can you make your CEM adaptive.
- Why CEM is not a onetime effort.

First we need to reiterate the importance of having a CEM that is modified in a timely fashion to the changes that occur in markets, environments, business practices, technology, geopolitical influences – in other words anything that affects the organization. Your risk management program needs to be in sync with your business. While this should be obvious it is unfortunately too often ignored.

Adaptive - In order to address the issues raised in a static CEM you need to adopt an approach that evolves with the changes that occur. We call this an adaptive approach.

To be adaptive an eCEM© needs to include:

- Periodic scans of technology, laws, regulations, intellectual property activity, internal operations and procedures, suppliers, competitors and customers to determine if any changes have occurred that will require changes to your CEM. Scans of suppliers and competitors are sometimes done as part of an organization's sales and marketing efforts and might be able to be used without major effort to include items relevant to CEM. As changes are identified they then need to be integrated into the CEM plan.

- Formal review mechanisms to make sure your CEM program is updated as part of your business strategic planning and done on a regular basis. To have credibility these reviews need to be at the board level.

- Exercises to make sure the procedures and processes to contain risks actually work. While many parts can be tested on a standalone basis, it is important to have an occasional broader test to verify that cross organization support is working properly.

- CEM itself must be a accessible, living breathing document. Some organizations are adapting the Wiki approach which allows collaboration, with editorial control, and easy accessibility.

The following are specific steps you should consider to make your CEM adaptive.

- Have a procedure in place that forces reviews and updates to your CEM. These reviews and updates need to be presented to the board level on a regular scheduled basis, at least semi-annually.

- Make sure the reviews include people with the most knowledge of the area under review. For example your information technology (IT) management should review the section of your CEM that addresses data center, network and program development exposures and risks. The reason for this is that IT managers should be aware of changes to operational procedures, new equipment, and processes.

- Make sure you have procedures in place so that when major events occur you can rapidly determine the impact on your organization. Resiliency will assure survivability.

- Make sure that all designated staff communicate events that impact their areas of expertise and responsibilities.

- Be sure the program includes provisions that staff duties include assessing and communicating the changes that occur in their area of responsibility.

- Make sure your reviews and scans examine and consider: new laws and regulations, new technologies, geopolitical events, extreme weather events.

- Make CEM reviews, awareness and reporting part of every employee's objectives.

- Make sure the reviews result in updates to your CEM.

- Require all parts of your organization to participate in your CEM program development, updates and reviews.

- Make sure your CEM is in a format that can be easily updated by all authorized, affected parties. There are multiple technologies that have emerged for this type of similar situations. For example the Wiki software, or Drop box.

In summary make sure your CEM evolves in step with all the changes that occur.

Chapter 3-10 – Measurement matters

"I often say that when you can measure what you are speaking about, and express it in numbers, you know something about it; but when you cannot express it in numbers, your knowledge is of a meager and unsatisfactory kind; it may be the beginning of knowledge, but you have scarcely, in your thoughts, advanced to the stage of science, whatever the matter may be."

> *Lord Kelvin from his 'Lecture on "Electrical Units of Measurement" (3 May 1883)*

In this chapter we will summarize why measurement matters and answer the following questions:

- What are the benefits of measurement?
- How can measurement improve your results?
- measurements, or metrics, can be used in an ERM program?

We believe there are ten good reasons why measurement matters.

1. **Measurement clarifies focus** - Faced with competing demands on their time and resources, what is measured gets attention – particularly when it is linked to rewards.

2. **Measurement defines expectations** - Measures are a primary means by which management can communicate its expectations to employees, in a clear and unambiguous manner.

3. **Measurement guides behavior** - People, especially at work, consciously or unconsciously operate on the basis of: "tell me how you are going to measure me, and I will tell you how I will behave."

4. **Measurement communicates performance** - If it's not being measured it will be ignored and no discussion can place regarding performance.

5. **Measurement improves decision-making** - One of the major causes of failure in decision-making is poor

or non-existent use of data. The right measure is worth a thousand opinions.

6. **Measurement increases objectivity -** Measurement is essential to "managing by fact" – otherwise you are left to lead with intangibles and subjective rationales for outcomes.

7. **Measurement improves execution** – What would the performance of baseball batters be like if batting averages were not measured. When outcomes are measured it is natural for people to try and improve, and those that don't are more easily identified.

8. **Measurement promotes consistency -** Unmeasured systems tend to be highly subjective with variable outcomes.

9. **Measurement provides feedback -** Timely, relevant measures allow individuals and organizations to determine if they are reaching their goals.

10. **Measurement promotes understanding**. Measures provide a communication channel allowing a very clear, common language to develop regarding desired outcomes and performance.

Metrics – The implementation and use of measures that describe an organization's CEM preparedness is critical to the success of any CEM program.

There are several key items you need to implement to make your CEM program effective.

- CEM metrics need to be integrated into the organizations objectives and reporting process.

- CEM metrics need to apply at all levels with metrics that relate to the specific job and responsibilities.

- CEM metrics need to include the risks the organization faces including likelihood and severity, preparations and plans in place, completion of plans, reviews and tests.

The graph on the next page is an example of a graphical summary of cyber risk.

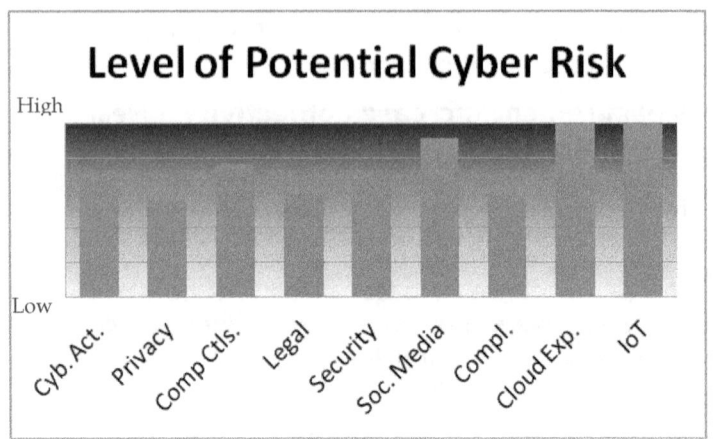

It provides a snap shot of the cyber exposure in key areas. Obviously this can be used to establish priorities and allocate resources. And, when used over time, can demonstrate progress or lack thereof.

In summary measurements are as necessary in cyber exposure management as they are in measuring other corporate objectives.

Chapter 3-11 – Making your Cyber Exposure Management effective - eCEM©

What questions will Chapter 3-11 answer for you?

- How do I get my organization to embrace cyber exposure management as an integral part of daily operations and not just a one off exercise?
- Can eCEM© really improve my business results (the bottom line)?
- If eCEM© is so economically valuable, why do we still read about cyber exposures becoming real on almost a daily basis?
- Do I really have to do this?

Let us answer each question in turn.

How do I get my organization to embrace cyber exposure management as an integral part of daily operations and not just a one off exercise?

> Because the management of risk is part of every operation and people are making cyber exposure management decisions every day without realizing it. What enterprise risk programs do is formalize the process.

> You also need to make sure your organizations culture embraces the need for cyber security. We recommend you consider the concepts put forth in Chapter 8 – Culture Matters.

Can eCEM© really improve my business results (the bottom line)?

> Yes, based on the reality that effective cyber exposure management will avoid, or lessen, the impact of events on your organization.

If eCEM© is so economically valuable, why do we still read about cyber exposures becoming real on almost a daily basis?

Because of the issues we have presented. If you examine the failures you will find the cyber exposure management programs, if there were any in place, were technology focused, generic, delegated down, and were not disciplined in their management.

Do I really have to do this?

If you do not make your cyber exposure management program broad in scope, integrated into your organization's culture, adaptive, and be able to measure your situation and accomplishments, you are wasting your resources, time and talent.

Now use the information presented in this book to make your organizations cyber exposure management program effective - an eCEM©.

About The Author

Doug Nagan has been actively involved in enterprise risk management and business continuity planning for the last fifteen years of his forty plus information technology and consulting career. Over the course of his career, Doug has helped clients, including the US Air Force, assess risks in manufacturing, finance, IT and supply chains. Results have included direct savings of over $100 million and the avoidance of potential risks of equivalent value through assessment of existing operational and implementing suggested improvements. His experience includes: business analysis, business continuity, information technology, merger consolidation, operations and process improvement, project and program management, risk management, and sourcing strategy. Clients include start-ups to Global 25 corporations across 8 industries.

Publications:

eERM – effective Enterprise Risk Management ISBN 978-1460980446
The Case for a National Preparedness Standard and Metric, presented at the IEE-HST conference in May 2007

Courses at the Global Risk Academy:

Understanding Cyber Exposures
http://globalriskacademy.com/p/cyber-exposure

Advanced Cyber Exposure Management (Parts 1 & 2)
http://globalriskacademy.com/p/cyber-exposure1
http://globalriskacademy.com/p/cyber-exposure2

GDPR Essentials for Risk Managers
  https://globalriskacademy.com/p/gdpr

Ransomware - A Crash course
  https://globalriskacademy.com/p/ransomware

Webinar: at Global Risk Academy

'Cyber wack-a-mole It is not a game'

Professional Associations
Life member IEEE and the Computer Society

Web Site has many more links and information

www,naganresearchgroup.com

Additional Reading

If you would like to know more regarding the concepts and background of the ideas presented in this book we suggest the following:

Books

The Black Swan, Nicolas Taleb, Random House, 2010

Organizational Culture and Leadership (fourth edition), Edgar H. Schein, John Wiley & Sons, 2010

Effective Enterprise Risk Management, Douglas A. Nagan 2013 ISBN 9781460980446

Standards: Example of widely accepted risk management standards are as follows. It should be noted that there are charges for many of their standards.

- ISO (http://www.coso.org/guidance.htm) ISO 27001/27002 are the international standards for technical risk management principles and guidelines.
- NIST Information Security Handbook: A Guide for Managers, http://csrc.nist.gov/publications/nistpubs/800-100/SP800-100-Mar07-2007.pdf

Personal Information: Guides from the US Government of protecting personal information.

- Protecting Personal Information: A Guide for Business, Federal Trade Commission, http://www.ftc.gov/infosecurity/
- Privacy Policies: Say What You Mean and Mean What You Say, Federal Trade Commission, http://www.ftc.gov/bcp/edu/pubs/articles/art09.shtm
- In Brief: The Financial Privacy Requirements of the Gramm-Leach-Bliley Act, http://www.ftc.gov/bcp/conline/pubs/buspubs/glbshort.shtm
- Information Compromise and the Risk of Identity Theft: Guidance for Your Business, Federal Trade Commission, http://www.ftc.gov/bcp/edu/pubs/business/idtheft/bus59.shtm

Cyber Threats: The following sites provide information regarding cyber threats.

- CERT National Cyber Alert System, http://www.us-cert.gov/cas/signup.html
- SANS Institute @RISK: The Consensus Security Alert, http://www.sans.org/newsletters/risk/?portal=6ea651380cdb76a250c69e382baf5c61
- FBI's Internet Crime Complaint Center: http://www.ic3.gov/default.aspx

Threat Assessment: An Introduction to Computer Security: The NIST Handbook Chapters 14 and 18, National Institute of Standards and Technology,

- http://csrc.nist.gov/publications/nistpubs/800-12/handbook.pdf
- Common Sense Guide to Prevention and Detection of Insider Threats, United States Computer Emergency Readiness Team, http://www.us-cert.gov/reading_room/
- An Introduction to Computer Security: The NIST Handbook, http://csrc.nist.gov/publications/nistpubs/800-12/handbook.pdf

---

[i] We are using the term 'business partner' to mean your suppliers, vendors, customers, financiers, bankers, sub-contractors and the like. Anyone who you interact with and whom you depend on for your organization to operate.

www.ingramcontent.com/pod-product-compliance
Lightning Source LLC
Chambersburg PA
CBHW051221170526
45166CB00005B/1991